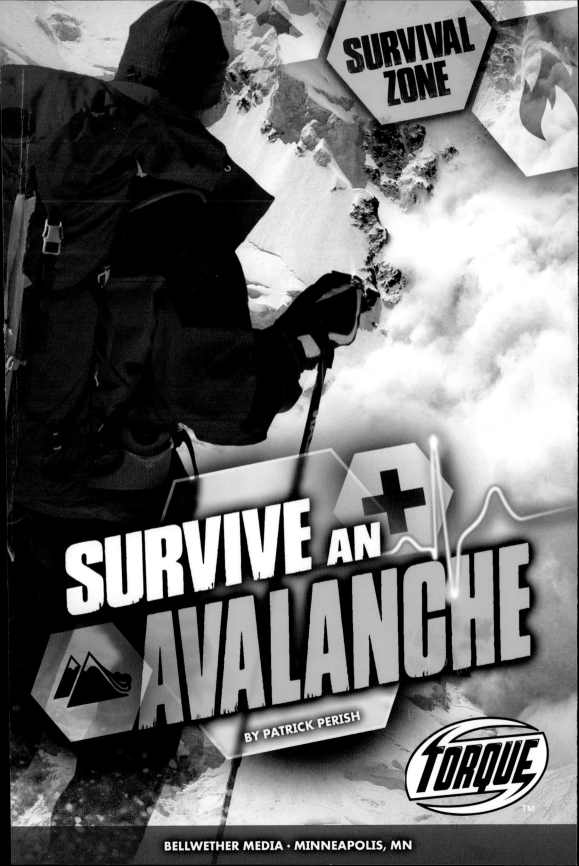

SURVIVAL
ZONE

SURVIVE AN
AVALANCHE

BY PATRICK PERISH

TORQUE™

BELLWETHER MEDIA · MINNEAPOLIS, MN

TM

Are you ready to take it to the
extreme? Torque books thrust you
into the action-packed world of
sports, vehicles, mystery, and
adventure. These books may include
dirt, smoke, fire, and chilling tales.
WARNING : read at your own risk.

This edition first published in 2017 by Bellwether Media, Inc.

No part of this publication may be reproduced in whole or in part without
written permission of the publisher. For information regarding permission,
write to Bellwether Media, Inc., Attention: Permissions Department,
5357 Penn Avenue South, Minneapolis, MN 55419.

Library of Congress Cataloging-in-Publication Data

Names: Perish, Patrick, author.
Title: Survive an Avalanche / by Patrick Perish.
Other titles: Survival Zone.
Description: Minneapolis, MN : Bellwether Media, Inc., 2017. | Series:
   Torque: Survival Zone | Includes bibliographical references and index.
   Audience: Ages 7-12. | Audience: Grades 3-7.
Identifiers: LCCN 2016034491 (print) | LCCN 2016046452 (ebook) | ISBN
   9781626175839 (hardcover : alk. paper) | ISBN 9781681033129 (ebook)
Subjects: LCSH: Avalanches–Juvenile literature. | Survival–Juvenile
   literature.
Classification: LCC QC929.A8 .P465 2016 (print) | LCC QC929.A8 (ebook) |
DDC 613.6/9–dc23
LC record available at https://lccn.loc.gov/2016034491

Editor: Christina Leaf   Designer: Jon Eppard

Printed in the United States of America, North Mankato, MN.

TABLE OF CONTENTS

Avalanche! _____ 4

The Making of an Avalanche __ 8

Surviving Disaster _____ 10

Gear Up and Get Smart _____ 12

A Deadly Trap _____ 16

To the Rescue! _____ 20

Glossary_____ 22

To Learn More _____ 23

Index _____ 24

AVALANCHE!

On February 28, 2014, a blizzard closed schools in Missoula, Montana. Coral Scoles-Coburn, age 10, was enjoying the snow day. She and her 8-year-old brother, Phoenix, were playing in the backyard. Suddenly, they heard a rumble.

High up on Mount Jumbo, a **mass** of snow broke free. It rapidly slid down the mountain. The kids had almost no time to react.

"I was outside with Phoenix when I heard the noise. I looked back at that mountain, and our backyard, and I just saw it coming."
-Coral Scoles-Coburn

neighbors searching for Phoenix

The snow and **debris** buried the children. Coral was able to pull herself free but Phoenix was trapped. Within

"I tried to lick and...bite my way out because I was too close together to get my hands out."
-Phoenix Scoles-Coburn

There was no sign of him under the snow. After more than an hour, a **probe** found Phoenix. He was rushed to the hospital. He had survived and soon healed completely!

THE MAKING OF AN AVALANCHE

Avalanches are huge masses of snow and debris moving down a mountain. Snow falling on a mountain piles up and forms a **snowpack**. Weak layers in the snowpack may break loose if disturbed.

Wind, falling rock, or a skier can set off avalanches. Small **sluff avalanches** occur when loose powder slides off the top. Dangerous **slab avalanches** happen when whole layers break off.

FORMATION AND PATH

heavy snowfall

heavy top layer

trigger

slab avalanche

weak bottom layer

FORMATION

starting zone

track

runout zone

PATH

SUDDEN DANGER

In five seconds, an avalanche can reach 80 miles (129 kilometers) per hour.

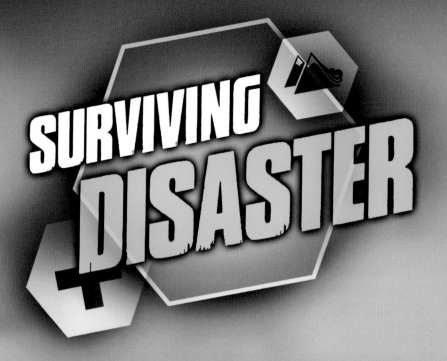

SURVIVING DISASTER

Avalanches can happen incredibly fast. But many are avoidable. Nine out of ten avalanche accidents are **triggered** by the **victims** or their group.

The best survival tip is to prepare. An avalanche survival course can teach important skills. Students learn to test snowpack and rescue victims. They practice traveling safely and checking conditions.

AVALANCHE DANGER LEVELS

Danger Level		Likelihood of Avalanches	
		NATURAL	HUMAN-TRIGGERED
EXTREME Avalanches certain. Stay clear of all avalanche terrain.		certain	certain
HIGH Very dangerous avalanche conditions. Travel through avalanche areas is not advised.		likely	very likely
CONSIDERABLE Dangerous avalanche conditions. Navigate terrain and find routes carefully.		possible	likely
MODERATE Some chance of avalanches. Study terrain and snow carefully.		unlikely	possible
LOW Mostly safe. Avalanches unlikely.		unlikely	unlikely

GEAR UP AND GET SMART

Before heading out for winter mountain activities, make sure you have the right gear. A few items could mean the difference between life and death.

A **beacon** will help rescuers locate you even if you are buried. An avalanche airbag can increase your chance of staying above the snow when the avalanche hits.

AVALANCHE SAFETY GEAR

beacon

avalanche airbag

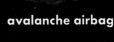

probe   slope meter   snow shovel

BOMBS AWAY!

Ski resorts use bombs to set off avalanches. They release the snow to make the slopes safe for visitors.

SAFETY IN NUMBERS

Always travel with a buddy. Cross risky ground separately. That way someone is ready to rescue if a slide happens.

Know how to tell if an avalanche is likely. Check **forecasts** put out by avalanche centers. Sunny spring days or days after heavy snowfall mean avalanches are more likely. High winds can increase slides, too.

Watch for warning signs. Cracks in the snow might mean it is unstable. Broken trees could signal previous avalanches. Learn to read the **terrain**. Use a **slope meter** to measure steepness.

slope meter

SLOPE DEGREES

Deadly avalanches are most likely on slopes around 35°. Snow and stress are able to build up. Steeper slopes have frequent but less dangerous avalanches. Avalanches are less common on gradual slopes.

50°
45°
40°
35°
30°
25°

90°

LOW DANGER
MODERATE DANGER
HIGHEST DANGER
MODERATE DANGER
LOW DANGER

0°

15

A DEADLY TRAP

If you are caught in an avalanche, you must act fast. Try to get off the slab. Skiers and snowboarders can try to pick up speed and shoot off to the side.

Try to grab a tree to keep yourself out of the avalanche. Use an avalanche airbag or swim to stay above the snow.

swimming

AVALANCHE AIRBAGS

In an avalanche, small objects get buried while larger objects rise to the surface. Avalanche airbags make you bigger. This gives you a better chance of staying near the top.

activates airbag

airbag inflates

victim rises to the surface

FLOAT

bca
backcountry access

As the snow slows, use your arms and hands to make an air pocket. Put an arm up to help rescuers find you. When the snow stops, it will set like concrete and trap everything in place.

probe

THE DEADLIEST AVALANCHE

In 1970, an earthquake set off a deadly avalanche in Peru. Towns were destroyed and around 20,000 people were killed.

Remain calm and try to breathe normally. Most avalanche deaths are caused by **suffocation**. Wait for rescue. Yell only if you hear rescuers nearby.

TO THE RESCUE!

If you see someone in an avalanche, pay attention to where they go down. Make sure another avalanche is unlikely before helping.

Carefully probe the snow for solid objects. Clothing or gear might offer clues. A shovel will make digging the victim out easier. Always be prepared. You may need to help someone survive an avalanche!

beacon—a device that gives off an electronic signal to help others locate it

debris—the remains of something broken down or destroyed

forecasts—predictions about certain conditions

mass—a large body of matter

probe—an instrument used for searching through snow

slab avalanches—avalanches in which the weak layer is lower in the snowpack and pulls upper layers with it; a slab avalanche falls as a thick, flat mass.

slope meter—a tool that measures the angle of a slope and shows the angles at which avalanches are more likely to occur

sluff avalanches—avalanches in which the weak layer is on top and slides off as a loose powder; sluff avalanches are less dangerous.

snowpack—snow that has collected and that covers an area

suffocation—the state of being unable to breathe

terrain—the land and its features

triggered—set off

victims—people who are hurt, killed, or made to suffer

AT THE LIBRARY

Lanier, Wendy. *Avalanches*. Minneapolis, Minn.: ABDO
Publishing Company, 2014.

Spilsbury, Richard. *The Science of Avalanches*. New York, N.Y.:
Gareth Stevens Pub., 2013.

Suen, Anastasia. *Avalanches*. Vero Beach, Fla.: Rourke Education
Media, 2015.

ON THE WEB

Learning more about
surviving an avalanche is as
easy as 1, 2, 3.

1. Go to www.factsurfer.com.

2. Enter "survive an avalanche" into the search box.

3. Click the "Surf" button and you will see a list of
related web sites.

With factsurfer.com, finding more
information is just a click away.

INDEX

avalanche airbags, 12, 13, 17

causes, 8, 10, 14, 19

dangers, 8, 11, 18, 19

debris, 6, 8

forecasts, 14

formation, 8, 9

gear, 7, 12, 13, 15, 17, 18, 21

likelihood, 11, 14, 20

Missoula, Montana, 4

Mount Jumbo, 4

mountain, 4, 8, 12

path, 9

Peru, 19

preparation, 10, 12, 14, 21

probe, 7, 13, 18, 21

quotes, 5, 7

rescue, 10, 12, 14, 18, 19, 20, 21

safety, 10, 12, 13, 14, 16, 17, 18, 19, 20

Scoles-Coburn, Coral, 4, 5, 6

Scoles-Coburn, Phoenix, 4, 6, 7

ski resorts, 13

slab, 8, 9, 16

slopes, 13, 15

snowpack, 8, 10, 15

speed, 9, 16

terrain, 11, 15

types, 8

warning signs, 15

The images in this book are reproduced through the courtesy of: Inu, front cover (subject); My Good Images, front cover (background), p. 5 (avalanche); dotshock, p. 5 (boy); Timothy Epp, p. 5 (trees); Associated Press, pp. 6-7; Lysogor Roman, p. 9; Jon Eppard, pp. 9 (infographic left, infographic right), 13 (beacon, probe, snow shovel), 15 (bottom), 17 (bottom left); Andrew Arseev, p. 11; Aurora Photos/ Alamy, pp. 12-13, 13 (slope meter), 15 (top); CNW Group/ Arc'Teryx/ Newscom, p. 13 (avalanche airbag); Adam Clark/ Getty Images, p. 14; SCPhotos/ Alamy, p. 16; Dorling Kindersley/ Getty Images, p. 17 (top); ZargonDesign, p. 17 (bottom right); Andia/ UIG/ Getty Images, p. 18; Helen H. Richardson/ The Denver Post/ Getty Images, p. 19; Ivan Chudakov, p. 20; Steve Smith/ Getty Images, p. 21.